WELCOME TO MY COUNTRY

Welcome to
PERU

Gareth Stevens Publishing
A WORLD ALMANAC EDUCATION GROUP COMPANY

Written by
DORA YIP/JANET HEISEY

Edited in USA by
ALAN WACHTEL

Designed by
JAILANI BASARI

Picture research by
SUSAN JANE MANUEL

First published in North America in 2002 by
Gareth Stevens Publishing
A World Almanac Education Group Company
330 West Olive Street, Suite 100
Milwaukee, WI 53212 USA

Please visit our web site:
www.garethstevens.com
For a free color catalog describing
Gareth Stevens' list of high-quality books
and multimedia programs, call
1-800-542-2595 (USA) or
1-800-461-9120 (CANADA).
Gareth Stevens Publishing's
Fax: (414) 332-3567.

© **TIMES MEDIA PRIVATE LIMITED 2002**
Originated and designed by
Times Editions
An imprint of Times Media Private Limited
A member of the Times Publishing Group
Times Centre, 1 New Industrial Road
Singapore 536196
http://www.timesone.com.sg/te

Library of Congress Cataloging-in-Publication Data
Yip, Dora.
Welcome to Peru / Dora Yip and Janet Heisey.
p. cm. — (Welcome to my country)
Includes bibliographical references and index.
Summary: An introduction to the country of Peru, including
information on its natural features, history, government, and
social life and customs.
ISBN 0-8368-2533-0 (lib. bdg.)
1. Peru—Juvenile literature. 2. Peru—Social life and customs—21st
century—Juvenile literature. [1. Peru.] I. Heisey, Janet. II. Title.
III. Series.
F3408.5.Y57 2002
985—dc21   2001042838

Printed in Malaysia

1 2 3 4 5 6 7 8 9 06 05 04 03 02

PICTURE CREDITS
Archive Photos: 14, 15 (bottom), 17, 36
Judi L. Baker: 40
Bes Stock: 3 (top)
Michele Burgess: 2, 20, 31
Focus Team: 6
Robert Fried: 4, 28, 32, 34
Eduardo Gil: 9 (top), 10, 21, 26, 35, 41,
    43, 45
Haga Library: Cover, 3 (bottom), 22, 33, 38,
    39
HBL Network: 13, 18
Dave G. Houser: 30
The Hutchison Library: 9 (bottom), 19, 23,
    24, 25, 27, 29, 37
North Wind Picture Archives: 11, 15 (top)
Michael J. Pettypool: 1, 16
South American Pictures: 5, 7, 8, 12
Tan Chung Lee: 3 (center)

Digital Scanning by Superskill Graphics Pte Ltd

Contents

Words that appear in the glossary are printed in **boldface** type the first time they occur in the text.

Welcome to Peru!

With mountains, lakes, deserts, and unexplored jungles, Peru is a land of **diversity** and beauty. Because the Incas set up their great empire in central Peru, some of the world's greatest **archaeological** treasures are found there. Let's learn about Peru, its people, and its unique culture!

Opposite: Students in the city of Cuzco chat in a city **plaza**.

Below: These children are from the town of Chachapoyas in Peru's north central highlands.

The Flag of Peru

Peru's national flag has a vertical white band between two red bands. White stands for peace and justice. Red stands for the blood of those who fought for freedom from Spain. The state flag (*right*) also has Peru's **coat of arms**.

5

The Land

Peru's area of 496,225 square miles (1,285,223 square kilometers) makes it South America's third-largest country. Bolivia, Brazil, and Colombia are east

of Peru, with Ecuador to the north, and Chile to the south. The Pacific Ocean borders the country's west coast.

Above: Lima is Peru's capital as well as its center of business and government.

With its coastal desert, the Andes mountain range, and the Amazon rain forest, Peru has three main geographic regions. The Andes separate the rain forest from the coastal desert. The rain forest covers most of the country.

Peru has many natural wonders. At 12,500 feet (3,810 meters) above sea level, Lake Titicaca is the world's

highest **navigable** lake. Colca Canyon is one of the world's deepest canyons. The Amazon River holds more water than any other river in the world. The highest mountain in Peru, Nevado Huascarán, is 22,205 feet (6,768 m).

Above: Peru's rain forest is home to thousands of plant and animal **species**, but few people live there. Some areas in this region are entirely untouched by humans.

Climate

Each of Peru's three regions has a different climate, and, instead of winter and summer, the seasons are "wet" and "dry." The warm coastal desert is always dry because the Andes block winds that bring rain from the Amazon region toward the coast. The dry season in the Andes is May to September. From October to April, this region has a lot of rain. The rain forest is wet all year round.

Left: People in the Amazon region live in houses built on stilts. The stilts keep the houses above flood waters during the region's wet season, from January to April. Rain in the dry season is not as often or as heavy.

Plants and Animals

Peru has a rich variety of animal life, including the famous condor, the world's largest flying bird, and **lamoids**, such as llamas, alpacas, and vicuñas. In fact, almost half of all the animal species in the world live in the Amazon rain forest — monkeys, jaguars, sloths, deer, and almost a thousand kinds of birds.

The rain forest has many plants, too, and the giant *Puya raimondii* is found only in the Andes. This plant's flower is a spike 30 feet (9 m) tall!

History

The first Peruvians probably came from Asia in about 1250 B.C. They settled in groups, and each group formed a different society. Some of the early societies were the Chimú, the Chavín, the Nazca, and the Inca.

The well-known Incas reigned in Peru from 1438 to 1533. In 1525, when Incan ruler Huayna Capac died, his two sons, Atahuallpa and Huascar, fought each other for control. Their **civil war** weakened the empire.

Below: Experts believe that thousands of laborers worked seventy years to build the fortress of Sacsayhuamán, which is located near the Incan capital of Cuzco. The Incas also built roads and temples, and they **irrigated** deserts and mountaintops.

Left: In 1532, led by Francisco Pizzaro, the Spanish kidnapped the Incan king, Atahuallpa. Although the Incas paid huge amounts of silver and gold for his release, the Spanish executed Atahuallpa in 1533.

When the Spanish arrived in 1532, Atahuallpa was ruler. The Spanish fought the Incas to capture their gold and silver, and they killed Atahuallpa. By 1535, the Incas were completely defeated. Spanish rulers were cruel to the **indigenous** and African peoples of Peru, thousands of whom died mining silver and gold for the Spanish king.

Independence

Peru declared its independence from Spain on July 28, 1821, but it was not fully independent until 1824, when Peru, Chile, and Venezuela finally defeated Spain. After Peru became independent, the country's economy grew rapidly, and a new railroad for transporting its rich resources to the coast made export much easier.

In the 1880s, land **disputes** led Peru to fight Chile in the War of the Pacific. Chile won a part of southern Peru, including the city of Lima.

Left: Owners of Peruvian rubber plantations treated their workers badly and paid them very poorly. Most of the workers were indigenous people.

Left: Soldiers searched voters during the 1990 election. They were on the lookout for **terrorists** because terrorist activities were common in the 1980s.

During the 1900s, Peru had more than twenty presidents. Many of them were **dictators** who treated the people badly. Although some of its presidents introduced **reforms**, Peru remained poor and unstable throughout the twentieth century.

In the early 1900s, some Peruvians formed labor unions and the American Popular Revolutionary Alliance (APRA) to fight for workers' rights. APRA is still an important political party in Peru today.

From Terrorism to Reform

In the 1980s, a terrorist group called *Sendero Luminoso*, or Shining Path, began attacks against government officials. Its leaders were finally arrested in 1992.

Elected president in 1990, Alberto Fujimori introduced strict economic reforms and made other changes in the government so nothing would block his reforms. The economy improved, but many people lost their jobs.

Below: In 1999, President Jamil Mahuad Witt (*right*) of Ecuador gave President Fujimori (*center*) a medal. Under Fujimori, Peru enjoyed very good relations with other nations.

Atahuallpa (1502–1533)

Atahuallpa was the last Incan ruler. Son of ruler Huayna Capac who died in 1525, he fought his half brother, Huáscar, for seven years before he became king in 1532. Atahuallpa was killed by the Spanish in 1533.

Atahuallpa

Andrés Avelino Cáceres (1833–1923)

When Chile conquered Lima in 1881, Andrés Avelino Cáceres, a Peruvian officer in the War of the Pacific, led a **resistance movement** that won back the country's capital. He was president of Peru from 1886 to 1890.

Javier Pérez de Cuéllar (1920–)

Javier Pérez de Cuéllar was Peru's first **ambassador** to the Soviet Union, in 1969, and was the United Nations secretary-general from 1982 to 1992. He played a key role in the **negotiations** that ended the Iran-Iraq war in 1988.

Javier Pérez de Cuéllar

Government and the Economy

Peru is a **republic** that is divided into twenty-four **departments** and one province. Each department reports to Peru's central government, which is led by the president. Laws are made by Congress, which has 120 elected members who serve five-year terms. Everyone from the ages of eighteen to seventy must vote.

Left: A changing of-the-guards ceremony is held daily at the government palace in Lima, Peru's capital city.

Left: In April 1998, Peru's special **commandos** held a ceremony to honor comrades who died in 1997 rescuing hostages held by terrorists at the Japanese embassy in Lima.

President Fujimori's Rule

From 1992, Alberto Fujimori ruled Peru as a dictator. He even changed the country's laws so he could run for a third term. Although reelected in April 2000, Fujimori resigned when he was accused of cheating in the election. A new president, Alejandro Toledo, was elected in June 2001.

The Military

Peru has a special antiterrorism unit in its military force of 125,000. Its skill in handling crises is known worldwide.

Industry and Agriculture

Lima is Peru's biggest industrial area. The country's major industries include petroleum, building materials, food processing, and mining. Peru's copper mines provide jobs for many people.

Many Peruvians work in fishing and agriculture, too. Peru is one of the world's biggest fish suppliers. Farmers grow rice, sugarcane, and cotton, but coffee is the main export crop.

Below: Salt is mined on ancient Incan terraces.

Left: Chili peppers are sun-dried after harvesting. They are commonly used in Peruvian dishes.

Natural Resources

Rich in natural **resources**, Peru is one of the world's top ten producers of silver, copper, lead, and zinc. The country's vast jungle regions provide oil, rubber, and wood. Peru's northern coast has large oil deposits, while natural gas is produced in the central part of the country's lowlands.

People and Lifestyle

Indigenous Peruvians are 45 percent of the country's population. Some of them speak only their native language. Because they do not speak Spanish, they are often left out of the country's economic progress. The largest groups of indigenous people are the Aymara in southeast Peru and the Quechua, most of whom live in the mountains. Other groups live in the jungles.

Below: These indigenous people celebrate a religious festival in Cuzco.

At 37 percent of the population, *mestizos* (mess-TEEZ-ohs) are the second largest ethnic group in Peru. Their ancestors are a mixture of indigenous people and Europeans.

The rest of Peru's people are Caucasians, Africans, Japanese, Chinese, and other groups.

21

Family Life

As with most other South Americans, the extended family is very important to Peruvians. The extended family includes aunts, uncles, cousins, and grandparents, as well as close family friends. Peruvians spend a lot of time with their families. They talk to each other about all family matters and make decisions together.

Below: Extended families in Peru get together often. This family is enjoying some refreshing fruit on a hot day.

Older family members involve children in daily activities. Through their support and guidance, they teach teenagers the value of family. Parents expect young adults to live with them until they marry. Some young couples even live with one set of parents after marriage. Women take care of the home, while men earn the family's income.

Above: A Quechua couple performs traditional rituals at their wedding in Cuzco.

Education

Most Peruvians over fifteen years old can read and write. Education is free, and children aged six to twelve must attend school. At the secondary school level, some choose not to go to school.

Schools run Monday through Friday, with a three-month summer vacation. Most schools use Spanish, but some rural schools use the local language.

Below: Students in rural areas may not attend school regularly because their families need their help at home or in the fields.

Higher Education

Peru has more than forty universities. The National Autonomous University of San Marcos, founded in 1551, is its oldest university. Many of Peru's universities are in Lima, but, because of the demand for higher education, twenty departments have their own universities. In villages and towns, graduates are well-respected and are often asked to settle disputes.

Above: Peruvian women see higher education as a way to gain society's respect as individuals.

Religion

The Spanish brought Catholicism to Peru. Today, most Peruvians are Catholics and observe Catholic customs. Masses are said in Spanish, Quechua, and Aymara, the most commonly used languages in Peru.

The number of **missionaries** in Peru is growing. Most of them are Protestants from North America.

Left: After the Spanish arrived in Peru, missionaries spread the Catholic faith throughout the country.

Many highland Peruvians worship nature. When the Spanish **denounced** these beliefs, the native people brought Catholic saints and symbols into their faith. Many crosses sitting on hills and mountains, for example, represent *apus* (AH-poohs), or mountain spirits.

Language

The three main languages spoken in Peru are Spanish, Quechua, and Aymara. Spanish and Quechua are Peru's official languages. Quechua was once the official language of the Incas. Aymara is an ancient language.

Spanish is the language most Peruvians speak outside their homes. With family members, they usually speak their local languages.

Below: Peruvians enjoy reading, and bookstands are a common sight in Lima.

Literature

Most early Peruvian writers wrote about the Spanish conquest of Peru. Later, César Vallejo (1892–1938), one of the greatest twentieth-century poets, focused on poverty and injustice. Ciro Alegría (1909–1967) was one of the first to write about the experiences of Peru's native people.

Flora Tristan (1803–1844), who had Peruvian roots, strongly supported women's and workers' rights in Peru. Her book, *Peregrinations of a Pariah*, describes her travels in the nation.

Arts

Ceramics and textiles were the main art forms in Peru before the Spanish arrived. The ancient Moche people made ceramics showing detailed scenes of daily life. Realistic faces in the scenes even showed different human feelings. Nazca and Paracas peoples were **weavers**. They made beautiful cloth with **intricate** designs that used up to 190 colors. Today, weavers are rediscovering these ancient techniques.

Left: Peruvians are very artistic, and many of them make handicrafts to sell to tourists.

Peru's great painters were part of the Cuzco school, a group of native artists who learned from Spanish and Italian teachers, but added indigenous details to their own paintings. One famous painting of the Last Supper shows Jesus and his apostles eating hot peppers and guinea pigs!

Architecture

Peru's buildings reflect its rich history. In Lima, modern buildings stand next to Spanish colonial buildings. The city of Cuzco has fascinating examples of Spanish and Incan **architecture**. Incan

Below: In Cuzco, many buildings are built on top of Incan stonework. The Incas placed stones, one on top of the other, without using any kind of cement to hold them together.

stonemasons were very skillful. Their building methods are still a mystery to modern engineers. The Incas carved and fitted together stones so well that, even today, a knife blade cannot be inserted between any two stones!

Music and Dance

Peruvians enjoy a wide range of music from the country's many different cultures. The most popular kinds of music are *huayno* (WHY-no), *saya* (SIGH-ah), and traditional folk music

from the Andes. African-Peruvian music, merengue, salsa, rock, and pop are also popular musical styles.

Peru's folk dancers combine many dance styles, and they often represent their country at international contests.

Above: These Quechua Indian children perform a dance during *Inti Raymi*, the Incan New Year. Many dancers belong to dance groups that perform at festivals and religious events.

Leisure

Peruvians like to spend time with each other, so their activities usually include friends and family members. Almost everyone in Peru likes to take *un paseo*

Below: Peruvians enjoy shopping at weekend flea markets, such as this one in Lima.

(UN pah-SAY-oh) — a walk. Especially in the evenings, people of all ages can be found strolling through city plazas.

Watching television is also popular in Peru. Some favorite programs are soap operas and sports, particularly soccer. In villages where electricity is scarce, the local government installs a television set in the main plaza.

In the cities, Peruvians enjoy eating out, shopping, going to the movies, and, in summer, going to the beach.

Sapo

Sapo (SAH-poh), or toad, is a Peruvian game. A metal toad sits on a box that has holes cut in it. Players throw disks at the holes and at the toad's mouth to earn points.

Above: Young skateboarders often get together to learn new techniques and to have fun with each other.

Sports

The people of Peru love soccer. One of the country's most famous players is Teófilo Cubillas, who started playing professional soccer at age sixteen. He played for Peru in the 1970 and 1978 World Cup contests and is one of the top ten goal scorers in World Cup history. In 1999, he became president of the Peruvian Sports Institute.

Below: In March 2000, Peru played Paraguay in a qualifying match leading to the World Cup in 2002. Here, the Peruvian soccer team lines up for a group photo before the match.

Volleyball is also popular in Peru. The Peruvian women's national team won a silver medal in the 1988 Olympics in Seoul, South Korea.

Water sports are popular on the coast. The village of Huanchaco, on the northern coast, holds an international surfing competition every year.

Above:
These children are playing volleyball at Sacsayhuamán, a huge fortress near Cuzco.

Festivals

All Peruvians celebrate the major Catholic holidays, and every village, town, and city also celebrates its patron saint's day with a festival that lasts three or four days. One church member, called the majordomo, is elected each year to plan events and raise money for this festival.

Semana Santa (say-MAHN-ah SAHN-tah), or Easter Holy Week, is one of the most important festivals in Peru. This Catholic festival lasts ten

Left: Colorful floats parade through village streets during Inti Raymi celebrations.

days. Each night, people carry statues and candles in a procession around the plaza and to each of the churches.

Inti Raymi, or the Festival of the Sun, is the Incan New Year. Indigenous Peruvians celebrate it each June with processions, dancing, and feasting.

Peru celebrates Independence Day on July 28, the day in 1821 when it declared its freedom from Spain.

Food

Peru's many ethnic groups, including Africans, Italians, Japanese, and even Chinese, as well as its varied climates, and different regions all influence the wide variety of food that Peruvians eat.

Left: *Pachamanca* (pah-chah-MAHN-kah) **is a traditional feast in the Andes. Meat and vegetables are cooked in a pit under hot stones, and whole families or villages come together to eat.**

Fish and seafood are commonly eaten on the coast. In the mountain regions, diets include chicken, beef, llama, and guinea pig. People in the jungle areas eat fruits, vegetables, freshwater fish, and rice.

Peruvians spice up all their food with *aji* (ah-HEE), which is made of hot peppers and lemon juice or oil.

Popular beverages include *chicha* (CHEE-chah), a traditional drink of corn, and Inca Kola, a sweet soft drink made from native fruits.

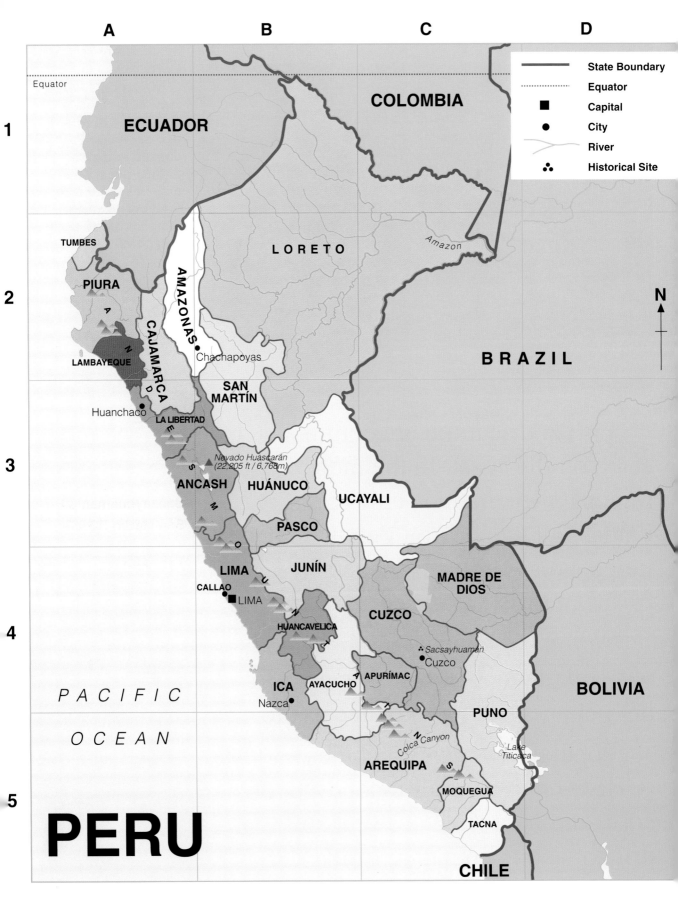

Above: Many buildings in Peru, such as these, are built on Incan foundations.

Amazon River
C2–D1
Amazonas A2–B2
Ancash A3–B3
Andes Mountains
A2–C5
Apurímac C4
Arequipa B5–C5
Ayacucho B4–C5

Bolivia D3–D5
Brazil C2–D3

Cajamarca A2–A3
Callao B4
Chachapoyas B2
Chile C5
Colca Canyon C5
Colombia B1–C2
Cuzco (city) C4

Cuzco (department)
C4

Ecuador A1–B1

Huancavelica B4
Huanchaco A3
Huánuco B3

Ica B4–B5

Junín B4

La Libertad A3–B3
Lambayeque A2
Lima (city) B4
Lima (department)
B3–B4
Loreto B1–C2

Madre de Dios C4

Moquegua C5

Nazca B4
Nevado Huascarán
B3

Pacific Ocean
A1–C5
Pasco B3
Piura A2

Puno C4–C5

Sacsayhuamán C4
San Martín B2–B3

Tacna C5
Titicaca, Lake
C5–D5
Tumbes A2

Ucayali B3–C3

43

Quick Facts

Official Name   República del Perú (Republic of Peru)

Capital   Lima

Official Languages   Spanish and Quechua

Population   27,012,899 (2000 estimate)

Land Area   496,225 square miles (1,285,223 square km)

Departments   Amazonas, Ancash, Apurímac, Arequipa, Ayacucho, Cajamarca, Callao (constitutional province), Cuzco, Huancavelica, Huánuco, Ica, Junín, La Libertad, Lambayeque, Lima, Loreto, Madre de Dios, Moquegua, Pasco, Piura, Puno, San Martín, Tacna, Tumbes, Ucayali

Highest Point   Nevado Huascarán 22,205 feet (6,768 m)

Longest River   Amazon River

Imports   Chemicals, foods, iron and steel, machinery, pharmaceuticals, transportation equipment

Exports   Coffee, copper, cotton, crude petroleum and byproducts, fish meal, lead, refined silver, zinc

Currency   Nuevo sol (S/. 3.63 = U.S. $1 as of 2001)

Opposite: Huanchaco fishermen use small boats made from bulrush reeds.

Glossary

ambassador: an official representing his or her country abroad.

archaeological: related to the study of the remains of ancient times and cultures.

architecture: a style of building.

civil war: a war between different groups within the same country.

coat of arms: a special shield that is a sign of a family or an institution.

commandos: members of military units that are trained to fight terrorists.

denounced: publicly called someone or something bad or evil.

departments: districts of a country with their own local governments.

dictators: rulers who have complete authority over a country.

disputes: arguments or quarrels.

diversity: many differences or much variety.

indigenous: native to a particular country or region.

intricate: complicated and detailed.

irrigated: supplied water to land using ditches, canals, and pipes.

lamoids: a family of animals related to the camel group.

missionaries: people who work to convert others to a religion.

navigable: suitable for boats to sail on.

negotiations: talks between groups with the goal of reaching agreement on a subject.

plaza: the town square, or open space for public use.

reforms: improvements.

republic: a country in which citizens elect their own lawmakers.

resistance movement: an organization that works to free a country from a foreign power.

resources: materials that bring wealth to a country.

species: a group of animals or plants that have similar habits and physical features and are considered to be of the same kind.

stonemasons: builders who shape stones or who build with stone.

terrorists: people who use random violence for political purposes.

weavers: craftspeople who work threads into a pattern to form a fabric.

More Books to Read

Chaska and the Golden Doll.
  Ellen Alexander (Arcade)

*Children of Peru. Through the Eyes of
  Children* series. Connie Bickman
  (Abdo and Daughters)

*The Llama's Secret: A Peruvian Legend.
  Legends of the World* series.
  Argentina Palacios (Troll)

*Macchu Picchu: The Story of the
  Amazing Inkas and Their City
  in the Clouds.* Elizabeth Mann
  (Mikaya Press)

Peru. Elaine Landau (Children's Press)

Peru. Countries of the World series.
  Kristen Thoennes (Bridgestone)

Peru. Festivals of the World series.
  Leslie Jermyn (Gareth Stevens)

Peru in Pictures. David A. Boehm,
  editor (Lerner Publications)

*Peru: Lost Cities, Found Hopes.
  Exploring Cultures of the World*
  series. David C. King
  (Benchmark Books)

Postcards from Peru. Denise Allard
  (Raintree/Steck Vaughn)

Videos

*Living Edens: Manu, Peru's Hidden
  Rain Forest.* (PBS Home Video)

Peru: Land of the Incas.
  (Choices, Inc.)

Peru: Spirits of the Amazon.
  (Wellspring Media)

Peru's City of Ghosts. (Discovery
  Home Video)

Web Sites

www.destination360.com/lostcities.htm

www.exploratorium.edu/learning_studio/
  news/february97.html

www.travelforkids.com/Funtodo/Peru/
  laketiticaca.htm

www.virtualperu.net

Due to the dynamic nature of the Internet, some web sites stay current longer than others. To find additional web sites, use reliable search engines with one or more of the following keywords to help you locate information about Peru. Keywords: *Amazon, Andes, Aymara, Cuzco, Inca, Lake Titicaca, Lima, Peru, Quechua.*

Index

DATE DUE